Bond

Non-verbal Reasoning

Assessment Papers

10–11⁺ years
Book 1

Alison Primrose

OXFORD
UNIVERSITY PRESS

Great Clarendon Street, Oxford, OX2 6DP, United Kingdom

Oxford University Press is a department of the University of Oxford. It furthers the University's objective of excellence in research, scholarship, and education by publishing worldwide. Oxford is a registered trade mark of Oxford University Press in the UK and in certain other countries

First published in 2002 by Nelson Thornes Ltd
This edition published in 2014

British Library Cataloguing in Publication Data
Data available

978-1-4085-2529-6

10 9 8 7 6 5 4 3 2 1

Printed in China

Acknowledgements

Page make-up: OKS Prepress, India
Illustrations: Bede Illustration

Before you get started

What is Bond?

This book is part of the Bond Assessment Papers series for non-verbal reasoning, which provides a **thorough and progressive course in non-verbal reasoning** from ages six to twelve. It builds up reasoning skills from book to book over the course of the series.

Bond's non-verbal reasoning resources are ideal preparation for the 11+ and other secondary school selection exams.

How does the scope of this book match real exam content?

Non-verbal Reasoning 10–11+ Book 1 and *Book 2* are the core Bond 11+ books. Each paper is **pitched at the level of a typical 11+ exam** and practises a wide range of questions drawn from the four distinct groups of non-verbal reasoning question types: identifying shapes, missing shapes, rotating shapes, coded shapes and logic. The papers are fully in line with 11+ and other selective exams for this age group but are designed to practise **a wider variety of skills and question types** than most other practice papers so that children are always challenged to think – and don't get bored repeating the same question type again and again. We believe that variety is the key to effective learning. It helps children 'think on their feet' and cope with the unexpected: it is surprising how often children come out of non-verbal reasoning exams having met question types they have not seen before.

What does the book contain?

- **6 papers** – each one contains 60 questions.

- **Tutorial links throughout –** 📖 – this icon appears in the margin next to the questions. It indicates links to the relevant section in *How to do ... 11+ Non-verbal Reasoning*, our invaluable subject guide that offers explanations and practice for all core question types.

- **Scoring devices** – there are score boxes at the end of each paper and a Progress Chart on page 64. The chart is a visual and motivating way for children to see how they are doing. It also turns the score into a percentage that can help decide what to do next.

- **Next Steps Planner** – advice on what to do after finishing the papers can be found on the inside back cover.

- **Answers** – located in an easily-removed central pull-out section.

How can you use this book?

One of the great strengths of Bond Assessment Papers is their flexibility. They can be used at home, in school and by tutors to:

- set **timed formal practice** tests – allow about 45 minutes per paper in line with standard 11+ demands. Reduce the suggested time limit by five minutes to practise working at speed.
- provide **bite-sized chunks** for regular practice
- **highlight strengths and weaknesses** in the core skills
- identify **individual needs**
- set **homework**
- follow **a complete 11+ preparation strategy** alongside *The Parents' Guide to the 11+* (see below).

It is best to start at the beginning and work though the papers in order. If you are using the book as part of a careful run-in to the 11+, we suggest that you also have two other essential Bond resources close at hand:

How to do ... 11+ Non-verbal Reasoning: the subject guide that explains all the question types practised in this book. Use the cross-reference icons to find the relevant sections.

The Parents' Guide to the 11+: the step-by-step guide to the whole 11+ experience. It clearly explains the 11+ process, provides guidance on how to assess children, helps you to set complete action plans for practice and explains how you can use the *Non-verbal Reasoning 10–11+ Book 1* and *Book 2* as part of a strategic run-in to the exam.

See the inside front cover for more details of these books.

What does your child's score mean and how can you improve it?

It is unfortunately impossible to guarantee that a child will pass the 11+ exam if they achieve a certain score on any practice book or paper. Success on the day depends on a host of factors, including the scores of the other children sitting the test. However, we can give some guidance on what a score indicates and how to improve it.

If children colour in the Progress Chart on page 64, this will give an idea of present performance in percentage terms. The Next Steps Planner inside the back cover will help you to decide what to do next to help a child progress. It is always valuable to go over wrong answers with children. If they are having trouble with any particular question type, follow the tutorial links to *How to do ... 11+ Non-verbal Reasoning* for step-by-step explanations and further practice.

Don't forget the website ... !

Visit www.bond11plus.co.uk for lots of advice, information and suggestions on everything to do with Bond, the 11+ and helping children to do their best.

Paper 1

Which shape on the right goes best with the shapes on the left? Circle the letter.

Example

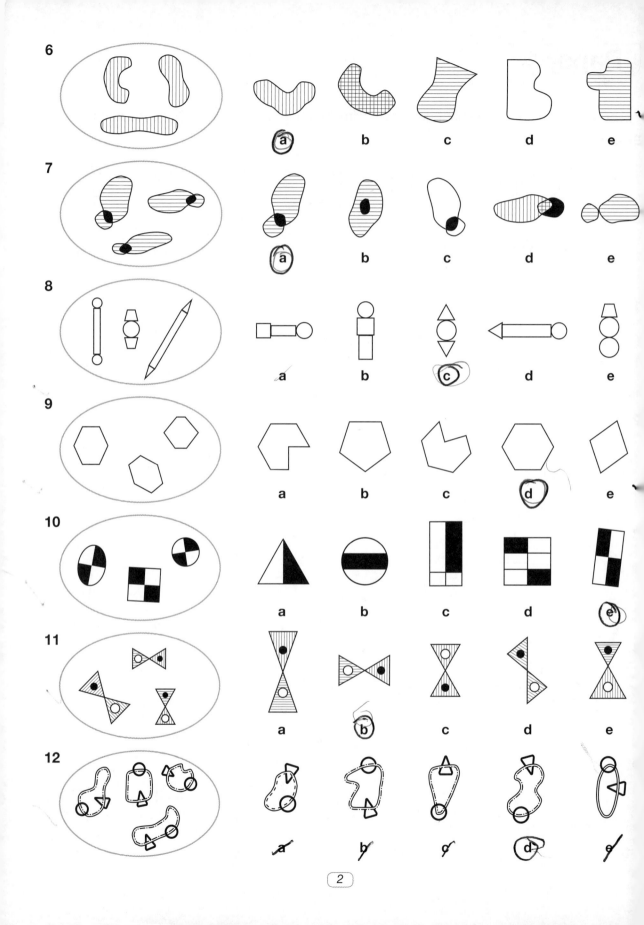

6

a b c d e

7

a b c d e

8

a b c d e

9

a b c d e

10

a b c d e

11

a b c d e

12

a b c d e

2

B 5 In which larger shape is the shape on the left hidden? Circle the letter.

Example

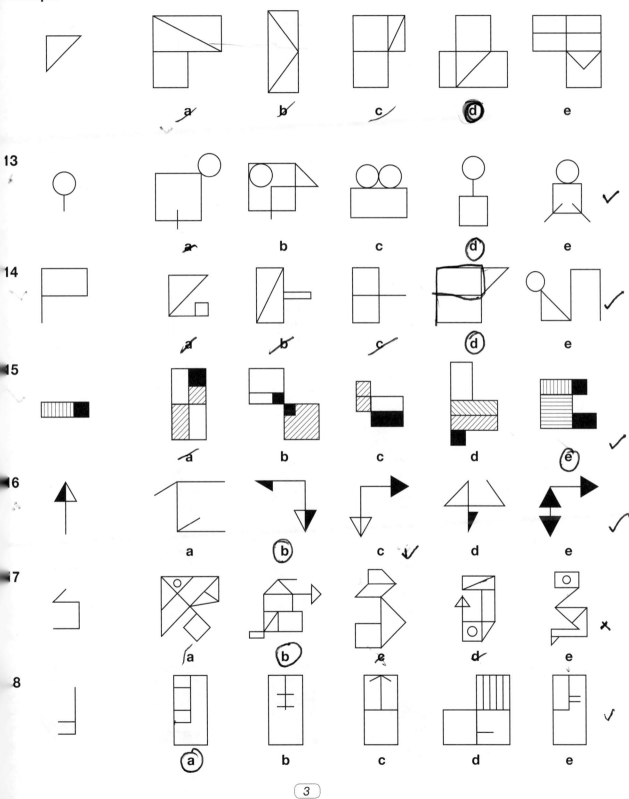

13

a b c d e

14

a b c d e

15

a b c d e

16

a b c d e

17

a b c d e

8

a b c d e

B 1 Which is the odd one out? Circle the letter.

Example

a   b   (c)   d   e

19

(a)   b   c   d   e

20

a   b   (c)   d   e

21

   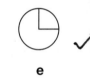

a   b   c   (d)   e

22

    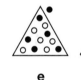

(a)   b   c   d   e

23

   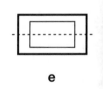

a   b   c   d   e

24

a   (b)   c   d   e

4

B 3 Which shape or pattern on the right completes the second pair in the same way as the first pair? Circle the letter.

Example

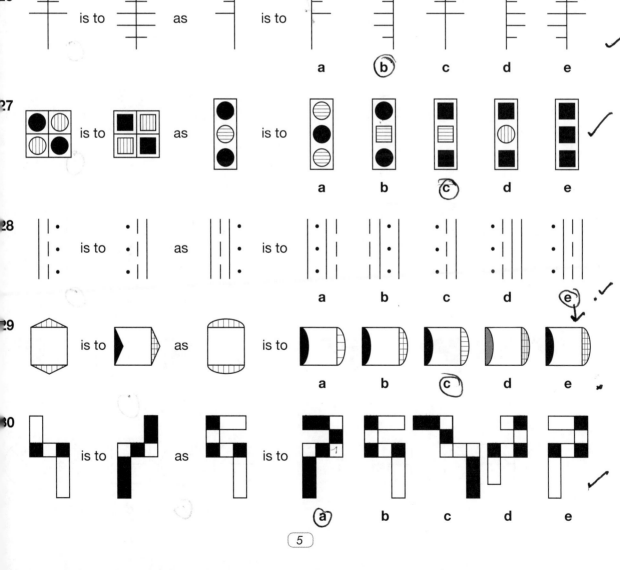

25   is to   as   is to
                a   b   c   d   e

26   is to   as   is to
                a   b   c   d   e

27   is to   as   is to
                a   b   c   d   e

28   is to   as   is to
                a   b   c   d   e

29   is to   as   is to
                a   b   c   d   e

30   is to   as   is to
                a   b   c   d   e

Which one comes next? Circle the letter.

Example

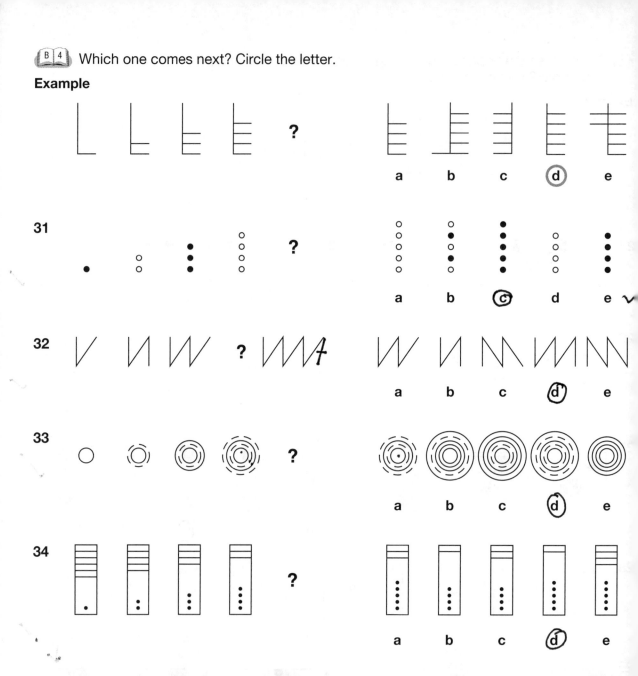

31

32

33

34

35

36

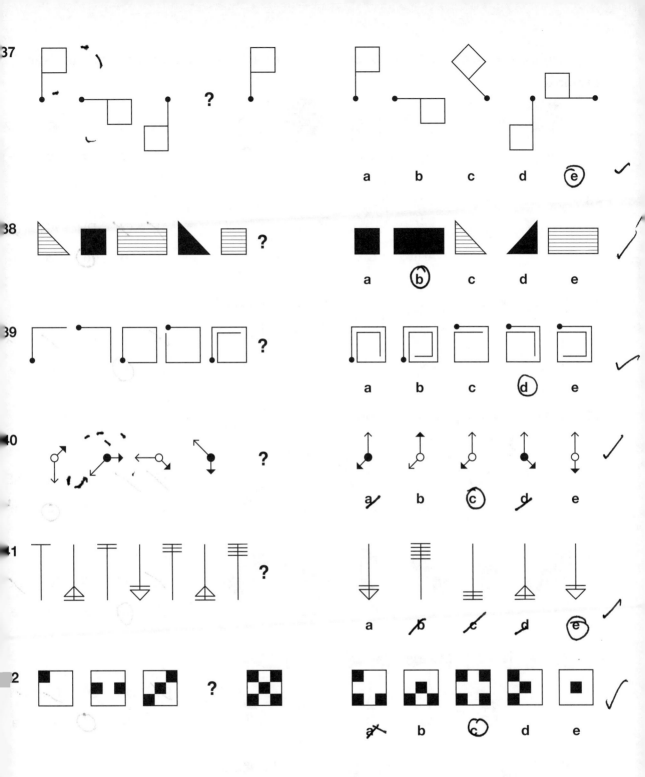

37 ?
a b c d (e) ✓

38 ?
a (b) c d e ✓

39 ?
a b c (d) e ✓

40 ?
a b (c) d e ✓

41 ?
a b c d (e) ✓

42 ?
a b (c) d e ✓

7

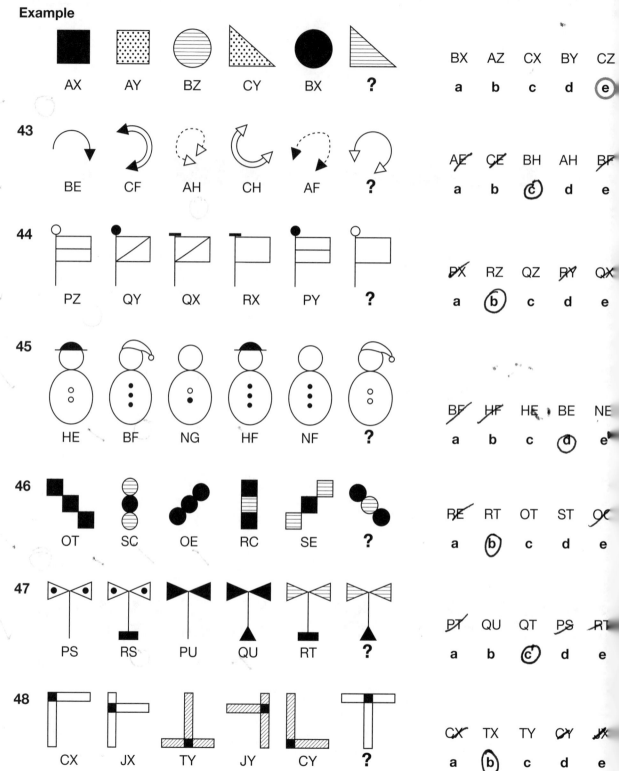

B 9 Which code matches the shape or pattern given at the end of each line? Circle the letter.

Example

AX   AY   BZ   CY   BX   **?**

BX   AZ   CX   BY   CZ
a   b   c   d   (e)

43

BE   CF   AH   CH   AF   **?**

AE   CE   BH   AH   BF
a   b   (c)   d   e

44

PZ   QY   QX   RX   PY   **?**

PX   RZ   QZ   PY   QX
a   (b)   c   d   e

45

HE   BF   NG   HF   NF   **?**

BF   HF   HE   BE   NE
a   b   c   (d)   e

46

OT   SC   OE   RC   SE   **?**

RE   RT   OT   ST   OC
a   (b)   c   d   e

47

PS   RS   PU   QU   RT   **?**

PT   QU   QT   PS   RT
a   b   (c)   d   e

48

CX   JX   TY   JY   CY   **?**

CX   TX   TY   CY   JX
a   (b)   c   d   e

8

Which shape or pattern completes the larger square? Circle the letter.

Example

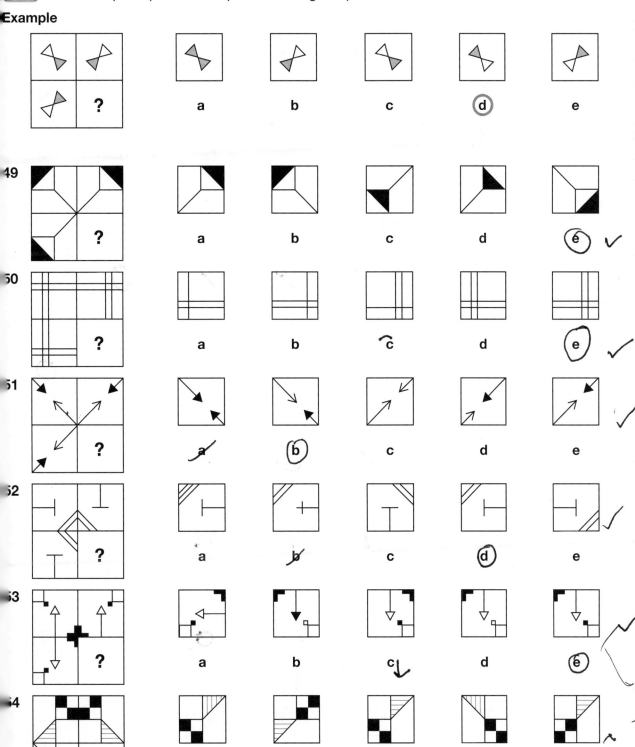

49

50

51

52

53

54

Which shape or pattern is made when the first two shapes or patterns are put together? Circle the letter.

Example

a   b   c   d   e

55   a   b   c   d   e

56   a   b   c   d   e

57   a   b   c   d   e

58   a   b   c   d   e

59   a   b   c   d   e

60   a   b   c   d   e

Paper 2

B 3 Which shape or pattern on the right completes the second pair in the same way as the first pair? Circle the letter.

Example

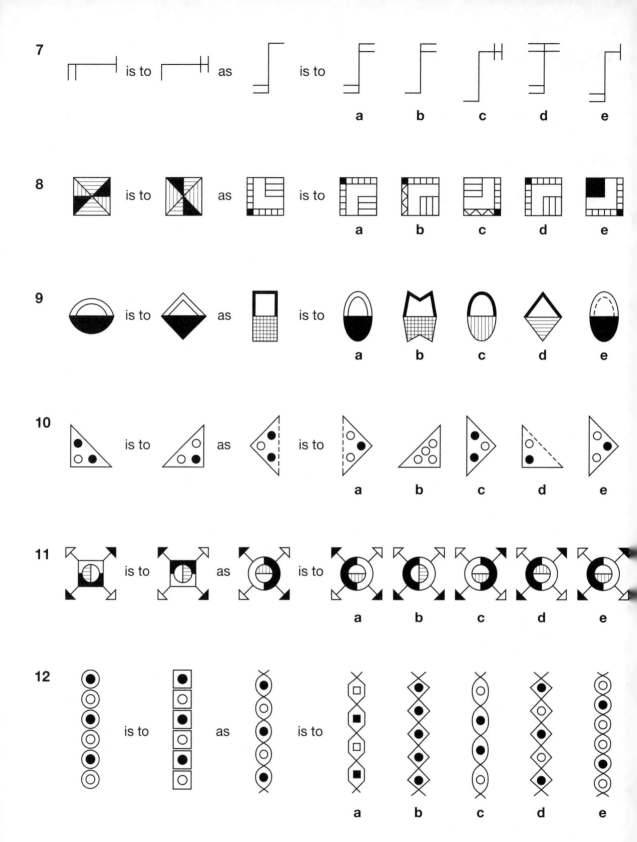

7

8

9

10

11

12

B 4   Which one comes next? Circle the letter.

Example

3

4

5

6

7

8

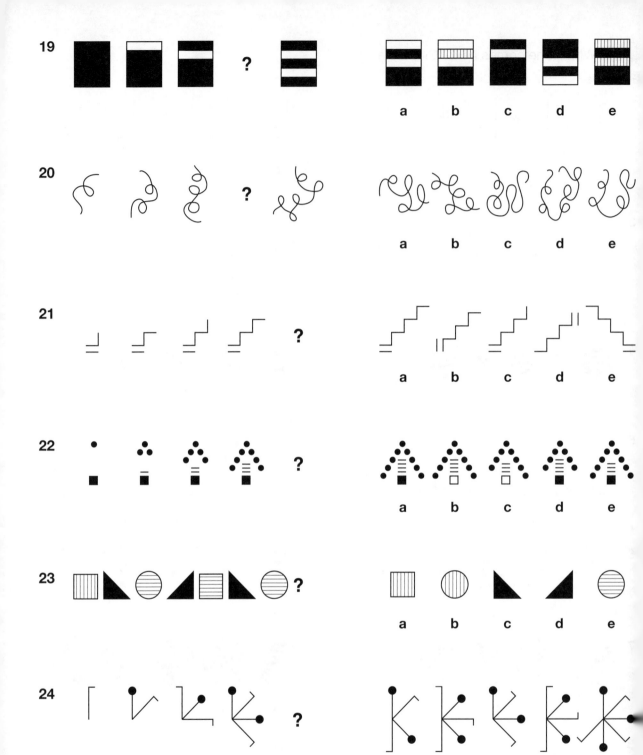

Which code matches the shape or pattern given at the end of each line? Circle the letter.

Example

	BX	AZ	CX	BY	CZ
	a	b	c	d	(e)

25

	SQ	SR	QR	QS	RS
	a	b	c	d	e

26

	XH	YJ	ZH	XP	YP
	a	b	c	d	e

27

	AW	PB	PD	FD	AB
	a	b	c	d	e

28

	KG	LF	ME	LG	KF
	a	b	c	d	e

29

	MZ	QZ	QY	MX	NZ
	a	b	c	d	e

30

	DR	TS	DP	ES	TR
	a	b	c	d	e

Which shape on the right goes best with the shapes on the left? Circle the letter.

Example

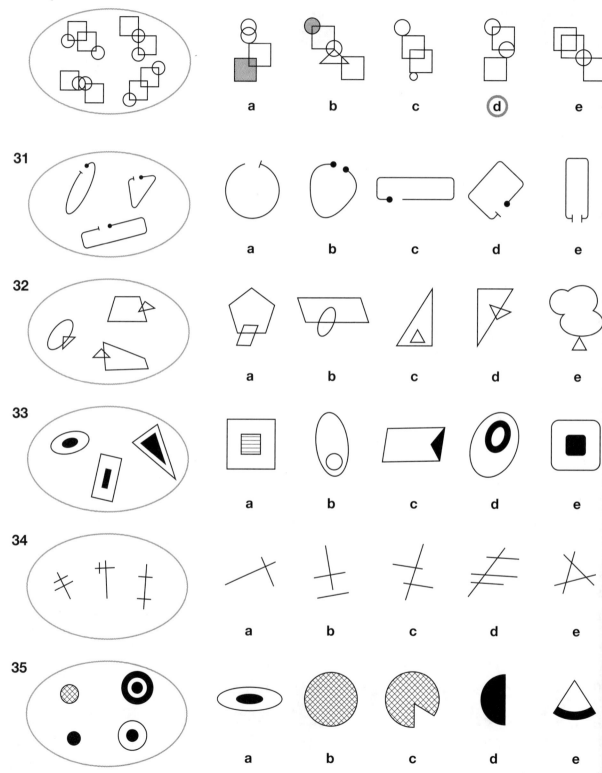

a   b   c   d   e

31

a   b   c   d   e

32

a   b   c   d   e

33

a   b   c   d   e

34

a   b   c   d   e

35

a   b   c   d   e

36

a b c d e

37

a b c d e

38

a b c d e

39

a b c d e

40

a b c d e

41

a b c d e

2

a b c d e

Which shape or pattern completes the larger square. Circle the letter.

Example

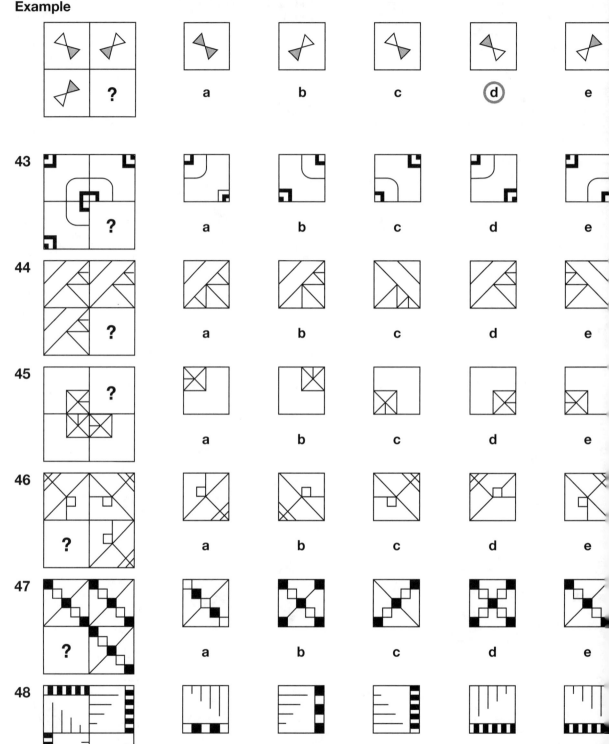

43

44

45

46

47

48

B 8 Which cube can be made from the given net? Circle the letter.

Example

49

a b c d e

50

a b c d e

51

a b c d e

52

a b c d e

53

a b c d e

54

a b c d e

Which shape on the right is the reflection of the shape given on the left?
Circle the letter.

Example

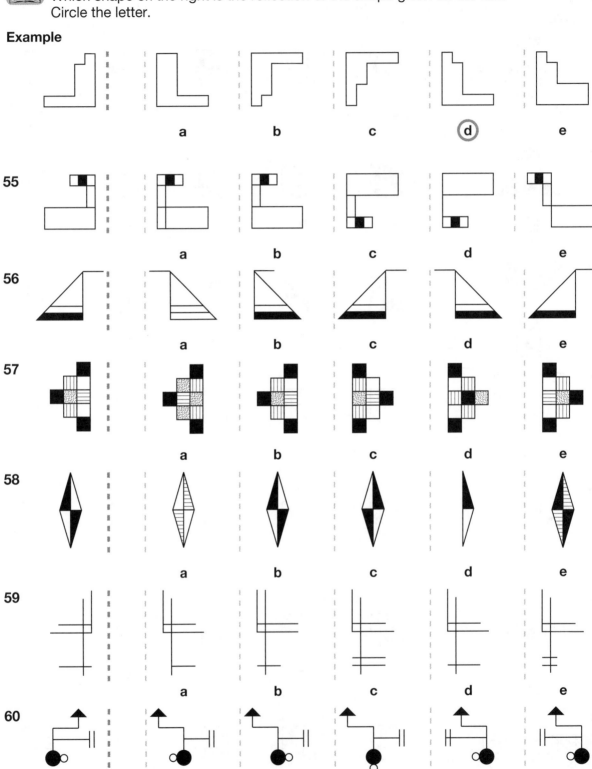

a   b   c   (d)   e

55

a   b   c   d   e

56

a   b   c   d   e

57

a   b   c   d   e

58

a   b   c   d   e

59

a   b   c   d   e

60

a   b   c   d   e

Paper 3

Which shape on the right goes best with the shapes on the left? Circle the letter.

Example

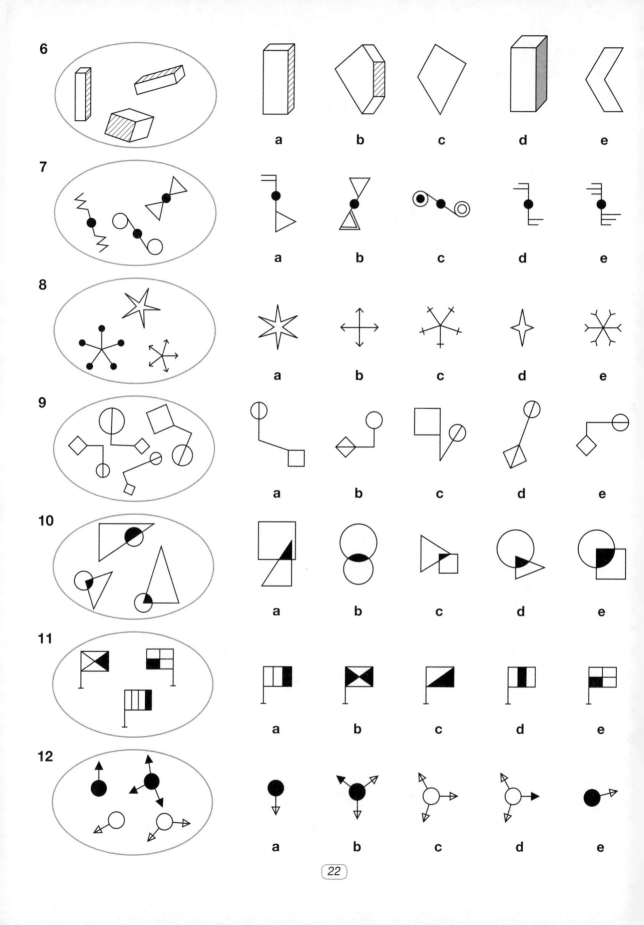

Which one comes next? Circle the letter.

Example

 ?

a   b   c   (d)   e

3

 ?

a   b   c   d   e

4

 ?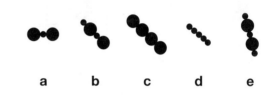

a   b   c   d   e

5

 ?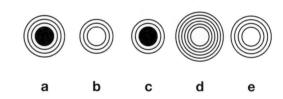

a   b   c   d   e

6

 ?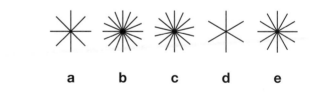

a   b   c   d   e

7

 ?

a   b   c   d   e

Which code matches the shape or pattern given at the end of each line.
Circle the letter.

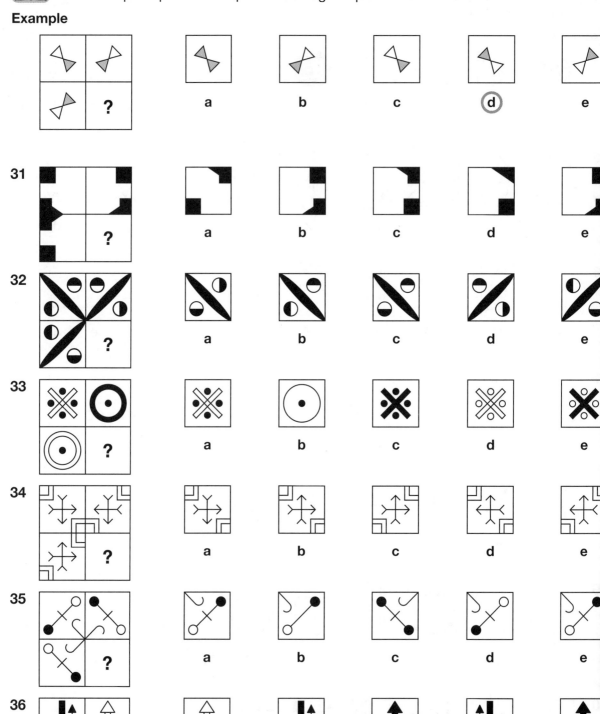

B 6 Which shape or pattern completes the larger square? Circle the letter.

Example

31

32

33

34

35

36

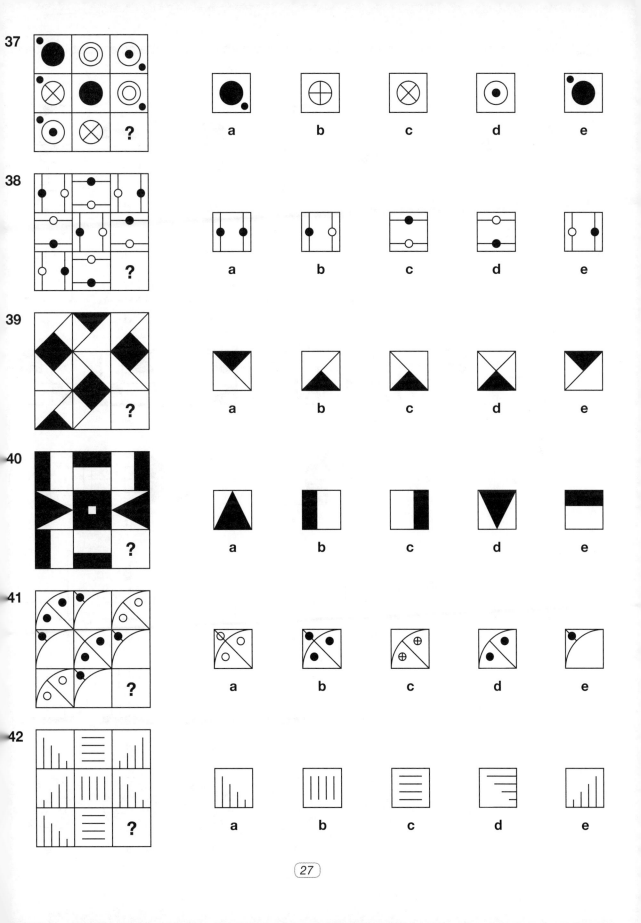

Which shape or pattern is made when the first two shapes or patterns are put together? Circle the letter.

Example

43

44

45

46

47

48

B 3 Which shape or pattern on the right completes the second pair in the same way as the first pair? Circle the letter.

Example

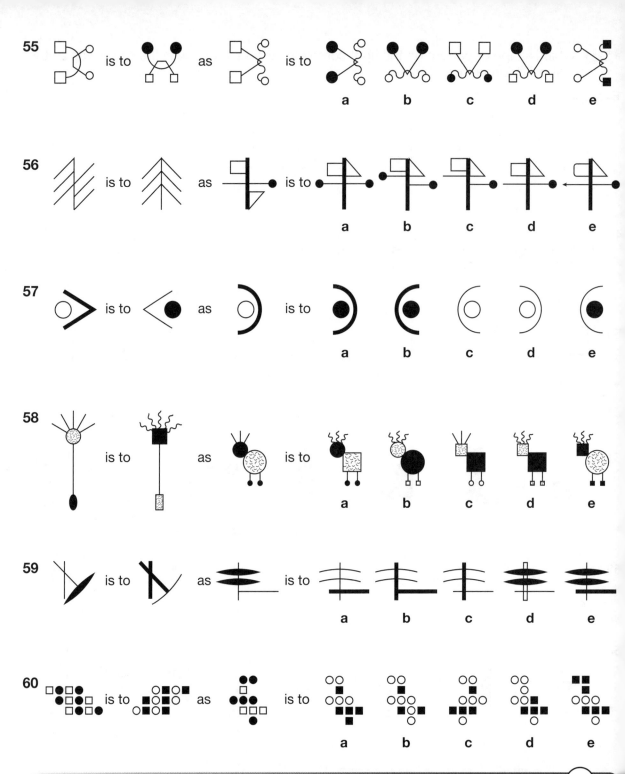

Now go to the Progress Chart to record your score!   Total   60

30

Paper 1		Paper 2	
1 a	31 c	1 b	31 d
2 b	32 d	2 c	32 d
3 c	33 d	3 b	33 e
4 e	34 d	4 a	34 c
5 c	35 c	5 a	35 b
6 a	36 b	6 c	36 d
7 a	37 e	7 b	37 c
8 c	38 b	8 d	38 e
9 d	39 d	9 b	39 c
10 e	40 c	10 a	40 c
11 b	41 e	11 e	41 e
12 d	42 c	12 d	42 e
13 d	43 c	13 c	43 d
14 d	44 b	14 e	44 d
15 e	45 d	15 c	45 c
16 b	46 b	16 b	46 b
17 c	47 c	17 b	47 e
18 a	48 b	18 e	48 e
19 d	49 e	19 a	49 c
20 c	50 e	20 a	50 e
21 d	51 b	21 c	51 c
22 e	52 d	22 a	52 a
23 b	53 e	23 d	53 d
24 b	54 c	24 d	54 c
25 e	55 d	25 b	55 b
26 b	56 e	26 e	56 d
27 c	57 b	27 b	57 e
28 e	58 c	28 d	58 c
29 e	59 e	29 e	59 d
30 a	60 b	30 b	60 e

Paper 3

1	d	31	c
2	e	32	a
3	e	33	c
4	b	34	d
5	b	35	e
6	a	36	e
7	d	37	a
8	c	38	b
9	e	39	b
10	d	40	c
11	e	41	d
12	c	42	e
13	e	43	d
14	b	44	b
15	e	45	e
16	e	46	b
17	c	47	e
18	b	48	d
19	c	49	c
20	d	50	e
21	d	51	c
22	d	52	a
23	b	53	a
24	e	54	c
25	d	55	d
26	c	56	d
27	d	57	e
28	c	58	d
29	a	59	b
30	e	60	c

Paper 4

1	e	31	d
2	c	32	c
3	b	33	a
4	c	34	d
5	d	35	c
6	d	36	d
7	d	37	a
8	c	38	d
9	e	39	d
10	a	40	e
11	e	41	b
12	b	42	e
13	c	43	d
14	d	44	d
15	b	45	c
16	c	46	b
17	b	47	e
18	a	48	e
19	e	49	a
20	a	50	d
21	b	51	c
22	e	52	a
23	d	53	c
24	e	54	d
25	b	55	d
26	e	56	e
27	e	57	d
28	c	58	c
29	d	59	e
30	d	60	d

Paper 5

1 c	31 e	1 b	31 b
2 d	32 d	2 c	32 c
3 e	33 d	3 d	33 d
4 a	34 c	4 d	34 c
5 c	35 d	5 c	35 c
6 b	36 a	6 d	36 d
7 d	37 c	7 b	37 a
8 e	38 e	8 a	38 b
9 d	39 e	9 a	39 e
10 c	40 e	10 b	40 a
11 c	41 e	11 c	41 e
12 a	42 c	12 e	42 e
13 b	43 a	13 c	43 b
14 c	44 e	14 d	44 d
15 e	45 e	15 e	45 e
16 b	46 d	16 c	46 c
17 e	47 a	17 b	47 a
18 e	48 e	18 c	48 e
19 c	49 b	19 d	49 e
20 c	50 e	20 e	50 d
21 d	51 c	21 d	51 e
22 d	52 e	22 b	52 e
23 b	53 d	23 d	53 c
24 c	54 e	24 b	54 c
25 a	55 c	25 a	55 e
26 a	56 e	26 d	56 d
27 e	57 d	27 b	57 d
28 b	58 d	28 d	58 d
29 b	59 d	29 d	59 b
30 d	60 b	30 e	60 a

The header "Paper 5" applies to the left two columns and "Paper 6" applies to the right two columns.

Paper 4

Which shape on the right goes best with the shapes on the left? Circle the letter.

Example

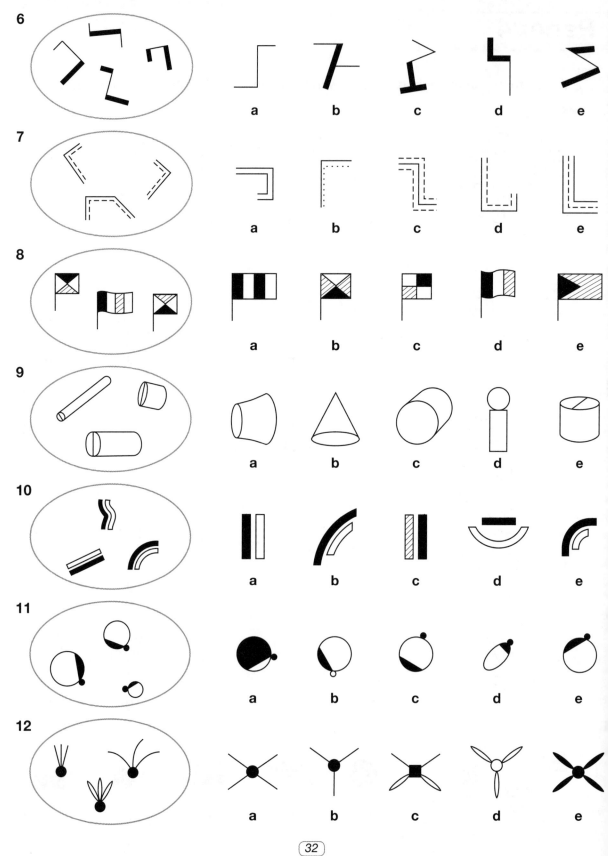

Which one comes next? Circle the letter.

Example

 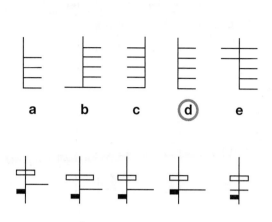

a   b   c   (d)   e

3

 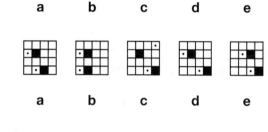

a   b   c   d   e

4

a   b   c   d   e

5

 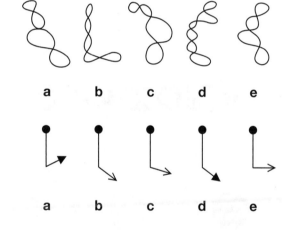

a   b   c   d   e

6

 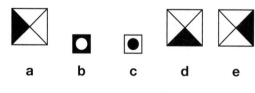

a   b   c   d   e

7

a   b   c   d   e

8

 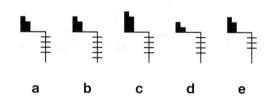

a   b   c   d   e

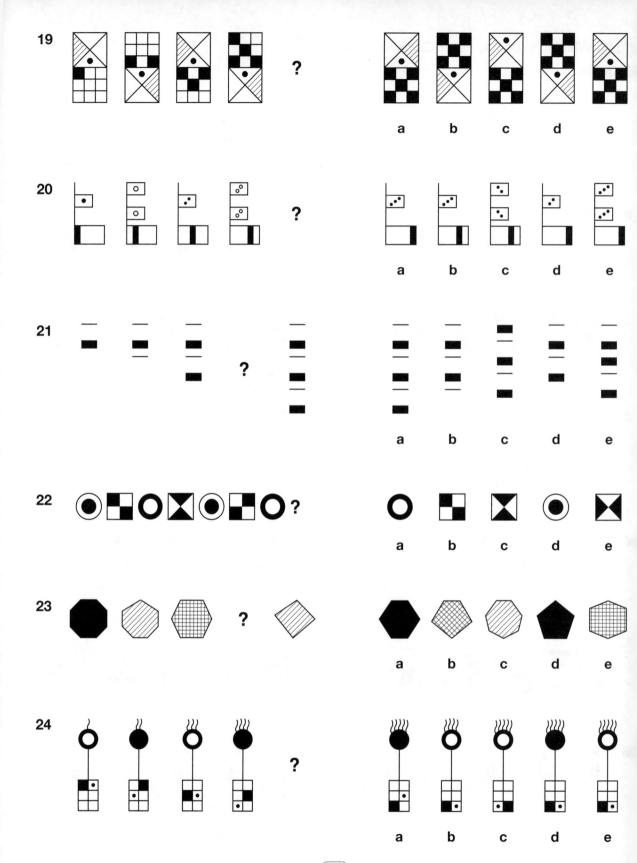

B 7 Which shape on the right is the reflection of the shape given on the left?
Circle the letter.

Example

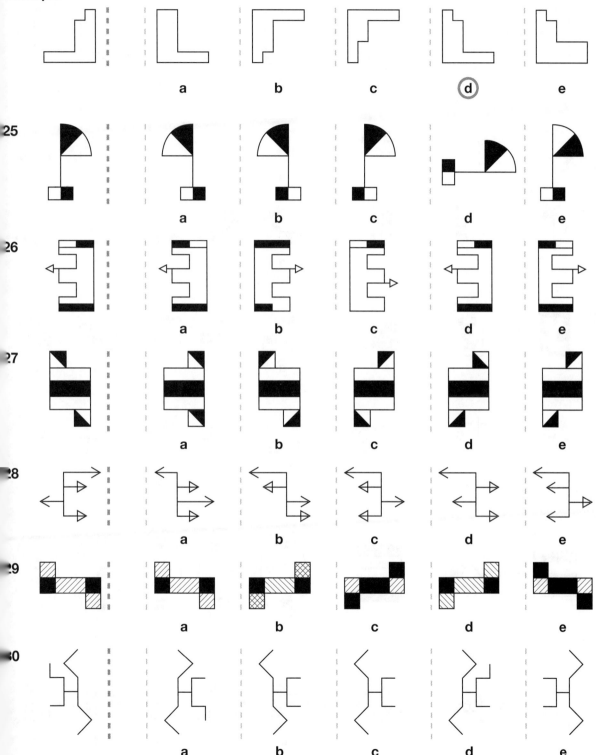

a   b   c   d   e

B3 Which shape or pattern on the right completes the second pair in the same way as the first pair? Circle the letter.

Example

31

32

33

34

35

36

Which shape or pattern completes the larger square? Circle the letter.

Example

43

44

45

46

47

48

a   b   c   d   e

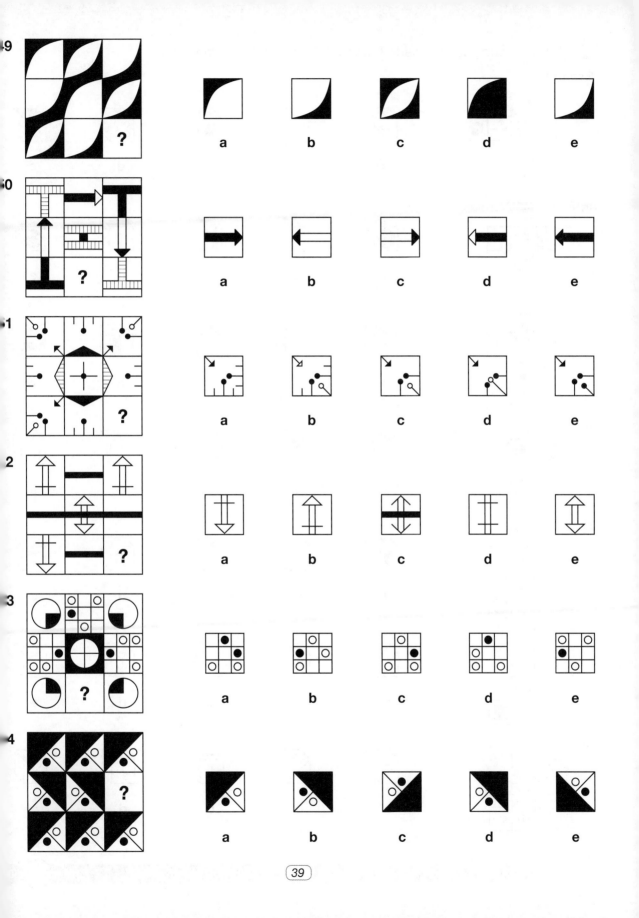

49

a b c d e

50

a b c d e

51

a b c d e

52

a b c d e

53

a b c d e

54

a b c d e

Which cube can be made from the given net? Circle the letter.

Example

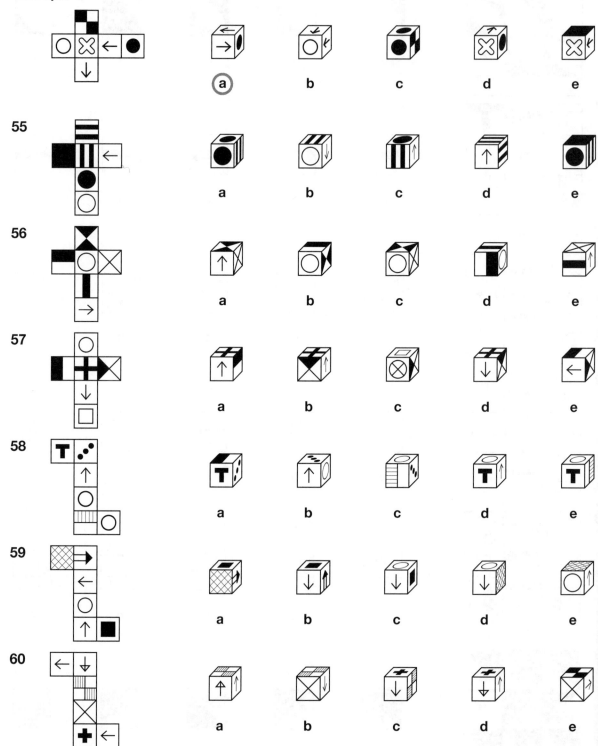

55

56

57

58

59

60

Paper 5

B 4 Which one comes next? Circle the letter.

Example

 ?

a   b   c   (d)   e

 ?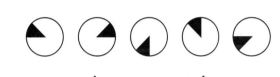

a   b   c   d   e

 ?

a   b   c   d   e

 ?

a   b   c   d   e

 ?

a   b   c   d   e

 ?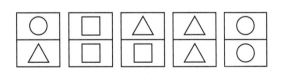

a   b   c   d   e

 ?

a   b   c   d   e

Which shape or pattern on the right completes the second pair in the same way as the first pair? Circle the letter.

Example

is to ___ as ___ is to

                a   **b**   **c**   **(d)**   **e**

13 is to ___ as ___ is to

                a   **b**   **c**   **d**   **e**

14 is to ___ as ___ is to

                a   **b**   **c**   **d**   **e**

15 is to ___ as ___ is to

                a   **b**   **c**   **d**   **e**

16 is to ___ as ___ is to

                a   **b**   **c**   **d**   **e**

7 is to ___ as ___ is to

                a   **b**   **c**   **d**   **e**

8 is to ___ as ___ is to

                a   **b**   **c**   **d**   **e**

19 is to ... as ... is to

a   b   c   d   e

20 is to ... as ... is to

a   b   c   d   e

21 is to ... as ... is to

a   b   c   d   e

22 is to ... as ... is to

a   b   c   d   e

23 is to ... as ... is to

a   b   c   d   e

24 is to ... as ... is to

a   b   c   d   e

B 9 Which code matches the shape or pattern given at the end of each line?
Circle the letter.

Example

	BX	AZ	CX	BY	CZ
	a	b	c	d	(e)

AX AY BZ CY BX **?**

25

	CA	AB	AC	BA	BC
	a	b	c	d	e

AC AB BA BC CB **?**

26

	YB	ZB	YC	XA	YA
	a	b	c	d	e

XA YA ZB ZB XC **?**

27

	TN	SN	UO	TO	UN
	a	b	c	d	e

SM TN UO TM SO **?**

28

	AZ	DZ	BZ	DY	CY
	a	b	c	d	e

AY BX CZ DX BY **?**

29

	SZ	SX	RY	TZ	TR
	a	b	c	d	e

RX SY RZ TY **?**

30

	KC	HB	JA	KB	HA
	a	b	c	d	e

HC JB KA JC HA **?**

B 2 Which shape on the right goes best with the shapes on the left? Circle the letter.

Example

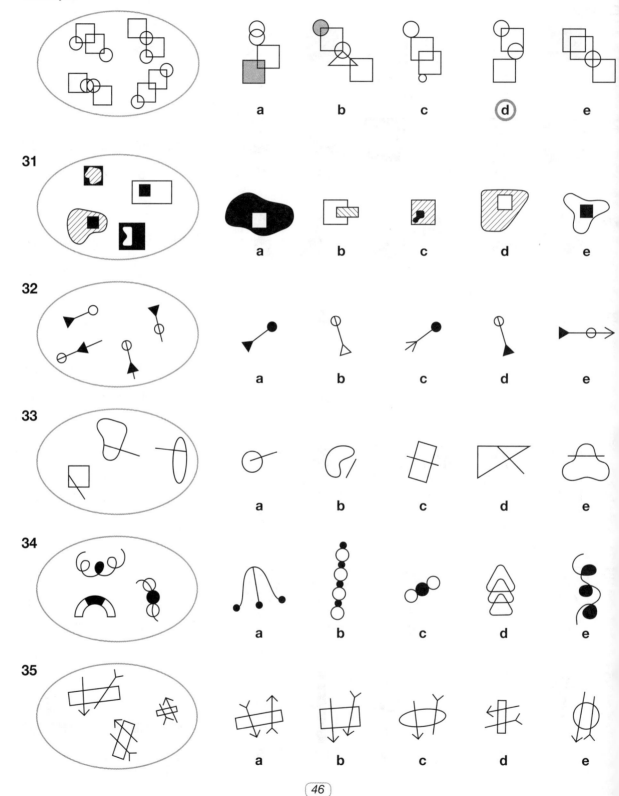

a   b   c   (d)   e

31

a   b   c   d   e

32

a   b   c   d   e

33

a   b   c   d   e

34

a   b   c   d   e

35

a   b   c   d   e

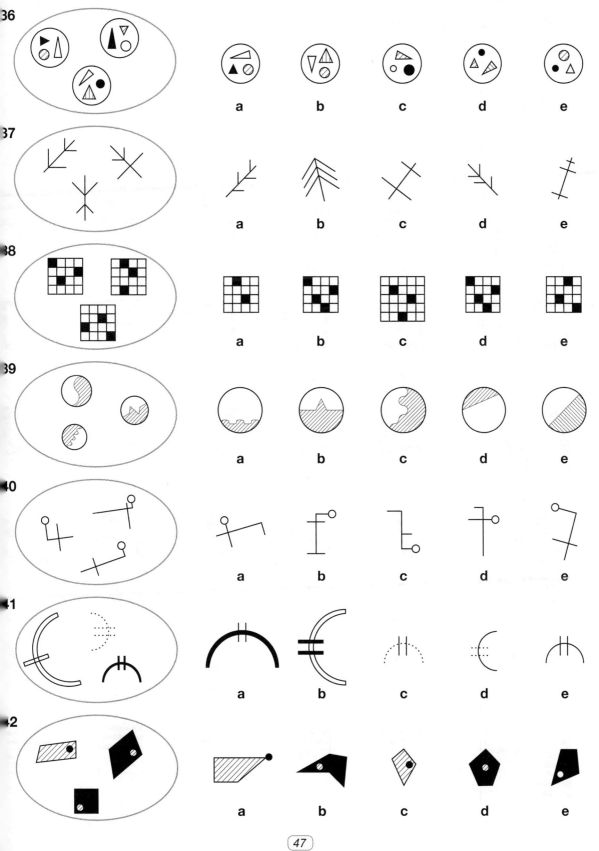

Which shape or pattern completes the larger square? Circle the letter.

Example

    a   b   c   (d)   e

43

    a   b   c   d   e

44

    a   b   c   d   e

45

    a   b   c   d   e

46

    a   b   c   d   e

47

    a   b   c   d   e

48

    a   b   c   d   e

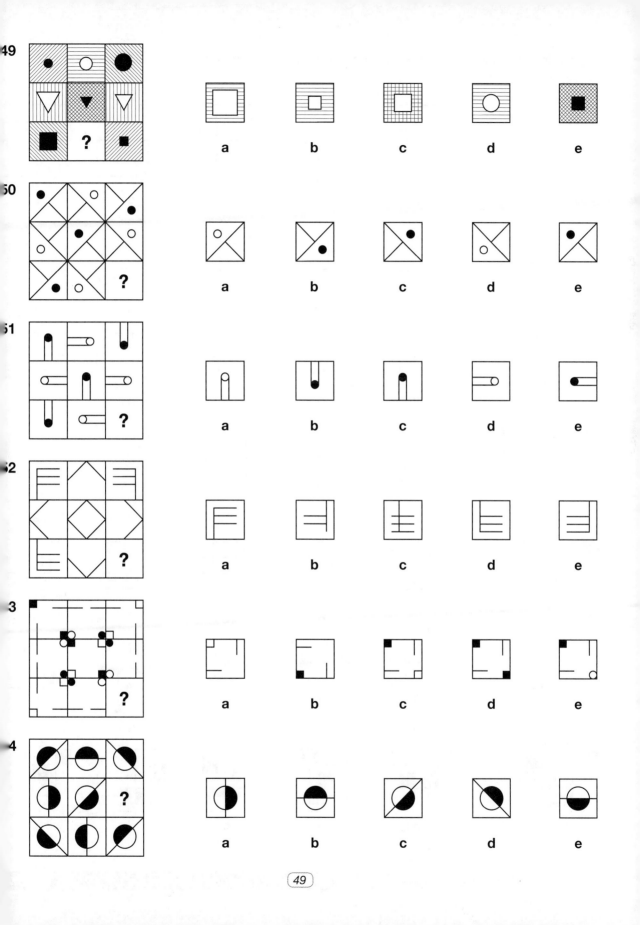

In which larger shape is the shape on the left hidden? Circle the letter.

Example

55

56

57

58

59

60

a   b   c   d   e

Paper 6

B 1 Which is the odd one out? Circle the letter.

Example

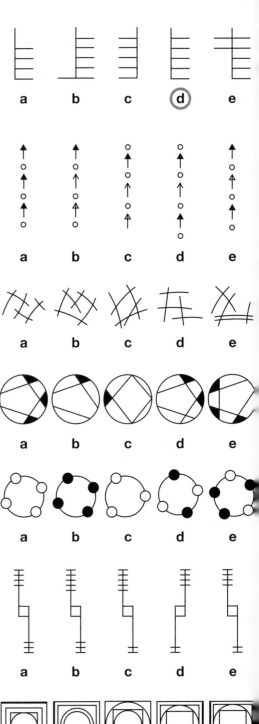

B 4 Which one comes next? Circle the letter.

Example

7

8

9

10

11

12

Which shape on the right goes best with the shapes on the left? Circle the letter.

Example

a   b   c   d   e

3

a   b   c   d   e

4

a   b   c   d   e

5

a   b   c   d   e

6

a   b   c   d   e

7

a   b   c   d   e

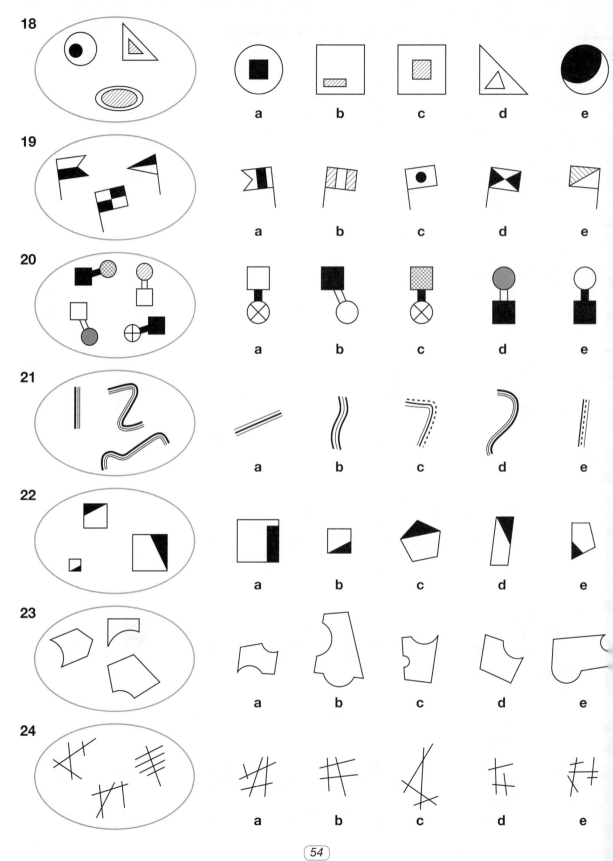

18

a b c d e

19

a b c d e

20

a b c d e

21

a b c d e

22

a b c d e

23

a b c d e

24

a b c d e

54

Which shape on the right is the reflection of the shape given on the left?
Circle the letter.

Example

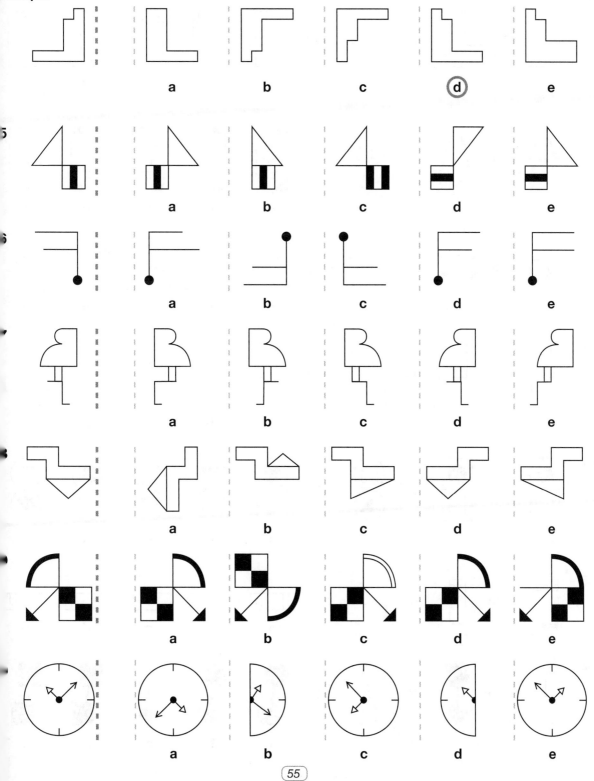

a   b   c   d   e

Which shape or pattern on the right completes the second pair in the same way as the first pair? Circle the letter.

Example

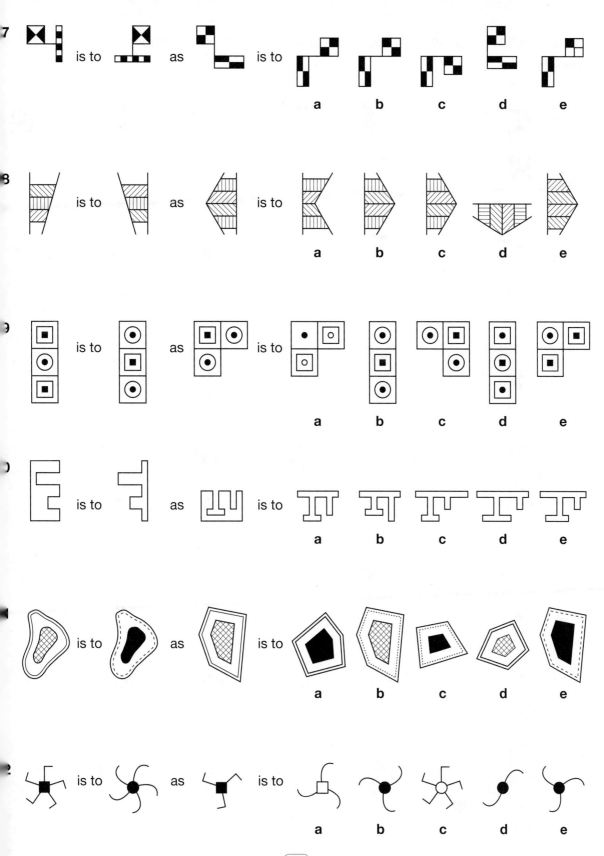

B 8 Which cube cannot be made from the given net? Circle the letter.

Example

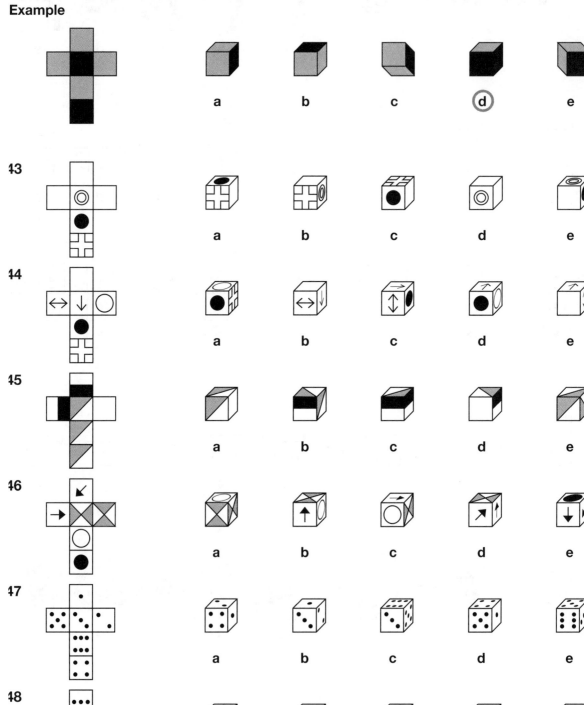

a   b   c   (d)   e

43

a   b   c   d   e

44

a   b   c   d   e

45

a   b   c   d   e

46

a   b   c   d   e

47

a   b   c   d   e

48

a   b   c   d   e

Which shape or pattern completes the larger square? Circle the letter.

Example

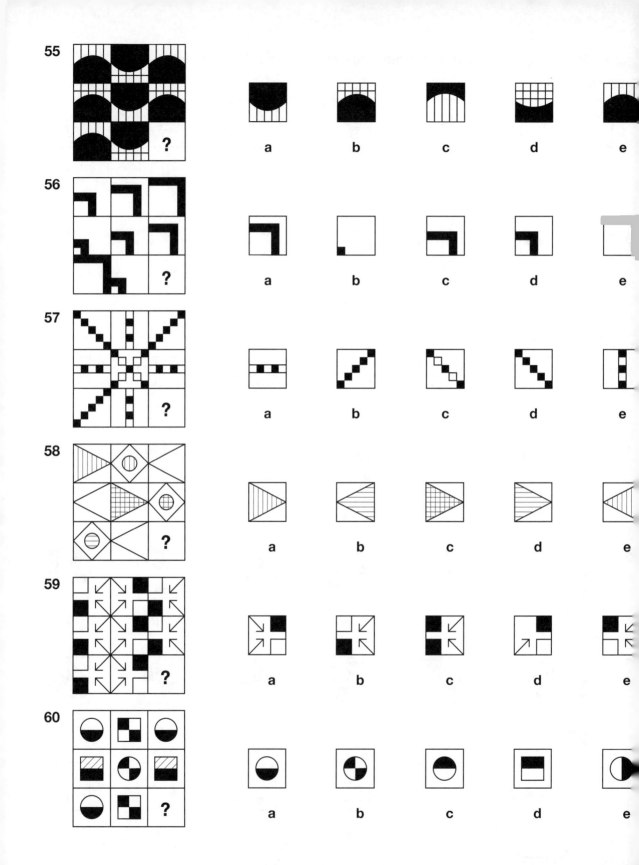

55

a   b   c   d   e

56

a   b   c   d   e

57

a   b   c   d   e

58

a   b   c   d   e

59

a   b   c   d   e

60

a   b   c   d   e

Progress Chart   Non-verbal Reasoning 10–11+ years Book 1

When you've finished the book use the Next Steps Planner